From co-author of *Never the Bride: a novel*

an inspirational devotional series

25 dates
with
God

volume three
falling
in love
with Jesus

cheryl mckay

www.dateswithGod.com
#dateswithGod

Books by Cheryl McKay

Never the Bride: a novel (with Rene Gutteridge)
Finally the Bride: Finding Hope While Waiting
Finally Fearless
Song of Springhill: a love story
Spirit of Springhill
Love's a Stage: a novel (with Rene Gutteridge)
O Little Town of Bethany: a novella (with Rene Gutteridge)
Greetings from the Flipside a novel (with Rene Gutteridge)
Wild & Wacky, Totally True Bible Stories Series (children's books with Frank Peretti)

Films / Videos / Audio Dramas by Cheryl McKay

The Ultimate Gift (screenplay by)
The Ultimate Life (screen story by)
Extraordinary (co-writer)
Indivisible (co-writer)
Gigi: God's Little Princess DVD (screenplay)
Superbook (episode writer)
RiverKids (audio show writer)
Wild & Wacky Totally True Bible Stories Series (audio show writer)

For Those Who Are Ready
To Fall Deeper in Love with Jesus

25 DATES WITH GOD:
Volume Three
Falling in Love With Jesus

Cover Photo: © ibush - Fotolia.com
Interior Chapter Graphics: © Pavel Sevcov- Fotolia.com
Cover Design by: Hope River Arts
Potter Illustrations: Peipei

Please exercise safety and caution when following any of the date
plans in this book. Author and Publisher assume no liability for
activities engaged in by readers of this book.

Published in the United States of America

Paperback:

ISBN-13: 978-1-946344-05-2

Copyright © 2019 by Cheryl McKay

First Edition 2019

TABLE OF CONTENTS

1 Peter 1:8-9
"Though you have not seen Him,
you love Him;
and even though you do not see Him now,
you believe in Him and are
filled with an inexpressible and glorious joy,
for you are receiving the end result
of your faith,
the salvation of your souls."

Welcome Back to Dates With God

$\mathcal{I}$ am so glad you're back for more. More dates, more romance, more time with the One who wants to continue that head-over-heels love relationship with you.

I hope by now you've completed the first two volumes' worth of dates. It's time for more. This installment is called *Falling in Love With Jesus*.

Specific to this edition, *most* dates can be enjoyed inside during winter or by doing activities outdoors appropriate for autumn. The prior editions had lots of outside nature dates. This edition helps supply date ideas for colder months, as fall and winter set in, so your dating relationship with our Lord doesn't have to get put on ice.

Just like before, I invite you to make "dating" part of your love story with Jesus. Go on a journey through the pages to come. Enjoy more dates that create and foster intimacy between you. This edition focuses on our love relationship with God's Son Jesus.

Jesus loves us so much. He wants to spend time with us. He is a true friend.

I hope by the end of this book you will continue to know this is true in the deepest parts of your heart and soul. I hope you will also grow in faith, in intimacy, and in the ability to sense Jesus' voice and companionship.

Let's review how this works before you begin. (If you don't need a review, go straight to Date 1.)

At the beginning of each date, I will give you a short guideline:

Location:
Supplies:
Reading:

Up front, I will let you know what location to choose. Sometimes, that may be as simple as "a quiet place." Other times, I'll get specific.

I'll also let you know what supplies to bring, like a journal, a Bible, art supplies, a camera. (Always assume you should bring this book with you, even if you leave it in the car sometimes. I won't include that on the list.)

Some dates require you to read the chapter in

advance. For others, you will read the chapter during the date. You just need to get the supplies outlined, then start the chapter once you're settled at the date's location.

Here are just a few additional guidelines. When experiencing these dates with Jesus, I encourage you to set aside electronics that are not specifically needed for the date. For safety, when away from home, bring your phone. Just consider using silent mode and keep it out of sight.

Spend time with the One you're dating, without letting the outside world distract you. Treat Jesus as you *should* treat a human date. For example, not letting your phone pull your attention at the dinner table. Save use of your phone to take photos, if that is your camera.

I'd love for you to take selfies or photos of sights Jesus shows you or speaks to you through while out on dates. These photos will tie into a future date. Plus, I want you to have something to share with the rest of us if you choose to participate through the hashtag:

#dateswithGod

If you use Twitter, also tag our handle: @purplepenworks. Share pictures, insights, or anything you want about Jesus meeting you on these dates.

Try to use just one journal for your dates so the notes you take during past dates will be with you. (If you already filled up that journal with Volume 1 or 2, start a fresh one.)

I hope you will record memories, moments, words exchanged between yourself and Jesus. Expect two-way communication. If you feel like the Lord speaks something to your heart, write it down. Capture your memories together.

Ready to go on dates with Jesus? Let's move on to Volume 3, Date 1.

Date 1
Put a Ring On It

Location: A quiet place at home
Supplies: A journal, a ring, necklace, or bracelet
Reading: Read chapter during your date

This book gives us the chance to focus on our relationship with Jesus, our Savior. Lover of our souls. That "Friend" who sticks closer than a brother.

If you have ever dated someone, were those dates more fun if you were friends with the person? Also, those who are married tend to have much more satisfying relationships if they are also friends with their spouse.

I normally start each book with asking my fellow daters, like you, to write a journal entry as a check-in to share where you currently are in your relationship with the Lord. This gives you a chance to have something to look back on 25 dates later to see how much you've grown. I still want you to do that on today's date.

But first, I have a different assignment to start with. I'm assuming most of us have heard this phrase: "Put a ring on it." It's commonly heard in reference to those wanting a commitment for marriage from the person they date.

If you're here for this third installment with dates with our Lord, I imagine you are committed. But how about, to kick this set off, we do something symbolic of that commitment?

Let's put a ring on it.

Now, you may already have a ring in your possession that you can use for this assignment. I also welcome you to find a bracelet or necklace. Find something you can use as a symbol of your dating relationship, your commitment to Jesus. Your commitment to spend time with Him. To grow your relationship even deeper than you have before.

I recently got a silver heart and cross necklace. It has an opening to put a lava rock inside, infused with the scent of an essential oil. Most commonly, I'll use frankincense. The heart is inscribed with the words, "I can do all things through Christ." It's a reminder for me, a great symbol specifically for this installment that focuses on Jesus. I try to remember to wear it especially when going on dates with Jesus.

Take a photo of yourself wearing the piece of jewelry of your choice, to add to your scrapbook when you finish this book of dates.

If you don't have something on hand you want to use, feel free to buy something special for this. During this date, go out to a store and find something special. (Jesus is one of few dates who won't complain about going to the mall with you.)

Before writing your opening love letter to Jesus, I'd like to give you a moment to ponder the most famous passage in Scripture about love. First Corinthians 13:1-13:

> "If I speak in the tongues of men or of angels, but do not have love, I am only a resounding gong or a clanging cymbal. [2] If I have the gift of prophecy and can fathom all mysteries and all knowledge, and if I

have a faith that can move mountains, but do not have love, I am nothing. 3 If I give all I possess to the poor and give over my body to hardship that I may boast, but do not have love, I gain nothing. 4 Love is patient, love is kind. It does not envy, it does not boast, it is not proud. 5 It does not dishonor others, it is not self-seeking, it is not easily angered, it keeps no record of wrongs. 6 Love does not delight in evil but rejoices with the truth. 7 It always protects, always trusts, always hopes, always perseveres. 8 Love never fails. But where there are prophecies, they will cease; where there are tongues, they will be stilled; where there is knowledge, it will pass away. 9 For we know in part and we prophesy in part, 10 but when completeness comes, what is in part disappears. 11 When I was a child, I talked like a child, I thought like a child, I reasoned like a child. When I became a man, I put the ways of childhood behind me. 12 For now we see only a reflection as in a mirror; then we shall see face to face. Now I know in part; then I shall know fully, even as I am fully known. 13 And now these three remain: faith, hope and love. But the greatest of these is love."

The Word gives us such specific guidelines on how we are to love. This comes across as loving selflessly. It may not sound like the most romantic love on the surface, but it's the best kind of love there is:

One that serves instead of looking to be served.

Next, I'd like to call attention to the all-important words of Jesus when He highlighted the two most important commandments:

"'Love the Lord your God with all your heart and with all your soul and with all your strength and with all your mind'; and, 'Love your neighbor as yourself.'" (Luke 10:27b)

It's all about this: *Love God. Love your neighbor.*

If we can do those two things, the rest of the commandments become easier to keep. For example, we won't lie, murder, steal, or covet the blessings of our neighbor if we love them. And naturally, loving God first helps us not sin against Him, not have any other gods before Him.

Now, for the rest of this date, take time to write a love letter to Jesus. Share with Him your dreams for this next round of dates with Him.

Dear Jesus:

My prayer for all who read this book is

they find a deeper love for You. Meet them where they are, Lord. Shower Your precious love upon them. We may crave earthly love, but no one loves us like You do. May our hunger for You be stronger than our desires for anything and anyone else. May we not want for anything that gets in the way of our fellowship with You.

Date 2
Campfire with Jesus

Location: A backyard with a fire pit, living room with
a fireplace, or a place with a grill, like public parks
Supplies: Paper and pen, matches, or lighter
Reading: Read chapter during your date

Many years ago, when I was an employee at The
Founders Inn in Virginia Beach, they had a spiritual
retreat for employees. One of the leaders took us
through a time of reflection that I've never forgotten.
The leader suggested we pray and ask if there were
anything standing between us and our intimacy with
Jesus. A sin, a stronghold, an idol. They gave each of
us a slip of paper and suggested we pray through
this question and write down anything the Lord

brought to mind.

I remember sitting there, reflecting, being aware of my flaws, yet still being aware there is forgiveness in Jesus and His shed blood on the cross. He died for those sins. But the act of confession is still important. If we don't acknowledge to Him that something is a sin, or take time to ask for His help in turning away from it, it feels like we are taking advantage of the grace He offers. It's like using that forgiveness as an excuse to live in sin. That's definitely not what He desires of us.

Sin interferes with intimacy with Jesus. The closer we get to Him, the more we desire to obey because we crave that deep fellowship. Fellowship can be broken when we put sin first. Sin prevents us from being as intimate as we could be if we weren't putting that sin (and the temporary pleasures of it) above our relationship with Him. So while it may seem like a less-than-romantic date activity, confession is actually quite romantic and will bring you closer to Jesus.

Before writing down your confessions, ponder these two verses:

> "If we will confess our sins, He is faithful and just and will forgive us our sins and to purify us from all unrighteousness." (1 John 1:9)

"Forgive us our sins, for we also forgive everyone who sins against us...." (Luke 11:4a.)

That second one is part of the famous Lord's Prayer, which reminds us how to pray. Our forgiveness of others is directly tied to God forgiving us.

So take some time with that blank sheet of paper before you. Ask Jesus to reveal anything you should write down in confession. Don't be afraid to put it in writing.

Then take time to make a list of anyone you feel you haven't forgiven for anything they've done against you.

Once you write down all of those things and feel satisfied that you've included everything, take some time to pray through each item.

Pray through forgiving others first.

Then acknowledge Jesus' sacrifice on the cross to die for those sins, and ask Jesus to forgive you. Truly repent. This includes the plan to turn away from that sin from now on.

Then comes the fun part I enjoyed most when I did this at The Founders Inn. It's time to burn that sheet of paper. Naturally, be safe, when and where you choose to do this. Only light this slip of paper on fire in appropriate places like in a fireplace, grill, or fire pit. They provided one with the exercise. But later, when I decided to do this exercise on my own, I used the tiny grill on my patio at Regent Village.

There's something about watching those "sins" written down burn up. I liked watching the words literally disappear. Any time I found myself tempted by the same sin, I'd remember that Jesus already forgave me for that sin. It was time to do my part and walk in obedience.

In middle school, they had a skit at chapel where there were two actors on stage. One played Jesus and one played a sinner. The sinner wrestled with asking forgiveness for a specific sin. He was sincere and the person playing Jesus spoke forgiveness for that sin after the sinner asked for it. Then, the sinner sat in silence, still wrestling with what he'd just confessed. Then, he said, "Jesus, about that sin…" And the actor playing Jesus asked, "What sin?"

Jesus changed the conversation.

The sinner hadn't changed the conversation, but Jesus had. The confession and forgiveness was complete. The skit was a neat illustration of how Jesus can let our sins go, even when sometimes it's hard for us to forgive ourselves. I was in seventh grade when I saw this skit, but I've never forgotten it.

So, the moral of the story is: once you confess, rest in your forgiveness by Jesus. Be ready to walk in obedience and not look back.

Now, if this is a sin that has been a long-time struggle and you find yourself wrestling deeply with ongoing temptations, consider finding an accountability partner in this.

Even though the exercise on this date is absolutely private, that doesn't mean if something is a tempting stronghold, you shouldn't consider confessing to a close friend. Or how about a family member, mentor, or pastor? Find someone who can hold you accountable in the future or check in to see how you're doing with a particular temptation. You can seek official counseling too.

If you find yourself struggling to let go of something that isn't necessarily sinful, you can utilize this same process of letting go. For example, if you experience a break up or the loss of an important dream, it may help to write that down and go through this symbolic act of letting go.

Anytime we clean the slate of what doesn't belong in our lives, we can go to our Lord with freedom of knowing we are forgiven, our sins covered by Jesus' extraordinary grace, and with our focus in the right place: on Jesus, our Savior and Friend.

Date 3
The Washing

Location: At home, a quiet place or bathroom

Supplies: A bucket, large bowl or tub, water, bath salts, soap, towel

Reading: Read chapter during your date

I hate feet.

Just ask my sister.

Our entire lives, I've hated to look at them, touch them, or especially feel her feet on me when she wasn't behaving. I certainly never wanted to wash someone else's feet. So, for me, Jesus washing the disciples' feet was the ultimate act of servanthood.

Think about how incredibly dirty feet were back

then! They walked endless days in sandals, down
dirt pathways. Think of the crud, the callouses. (On
second thought, don't. That's gross.)

Since we got confession out of the way on the
prior date, now is a nice chance to follow with a date
that includes washing feet. But don't worry. Unless
you feel strongly about doing this date with a fellow
Dates With God pal, this date is just between you and
Jesus. No outside feet involved.

So gather a bucket or a large plastic bowl. You
can sit on the edge of your tub if you'd like. Get
some Epsom bath salts if your skin is okay with
them, bubble bath, and soap. (Fizzling bath bombs
can be fun too. Just break off a small portion for your
feet.)

Before putting water in that tub or bucket, take
the time to meditate on the following Scripture
passage from John 13:1-17:

> "It was just before the Passover
> Festival. Jesus knew that the hour had
> come for Him to leave this world and go to
> the Father. Having loved His own who
> were in the world, He loved them to the
> end. ² The evening meal was in progress,
> and the devil had already prompted Judas,
> the son of Simon Iscariot, to betray
> Jesus. ³ Jesus knew that the Father had put
> all things under His power, and that He

had come from God and was returning to God; ⁴ so He got up from the meal, took off His outer clothing, and wrapped a towel around His waist. ⁵ After that, He poured water into a basin and began to wash His disciples' feet, drying them with the towel that was wrapped around Him. ⁶ He came to Simon Peter, who said to Him, 'Lord, are you going to wash my feet?' ⁷ Jesus replied, 'You do not realize now what I am doing, but later you will understand.' ⁸ 'No,' said Peter, 'you shall never wash my feet.' Jesus answered, 'Unless I wash you, you have no part with Me.' ⁹ 'Then, Lord,' Simon Peter replied, 'not just my feet but my hands and my head as well!' ¹⁰ Jesus answered, 'Those who have had a bath need only to wash their feet; their whole body is clean. And you are clean, though not every one of you.' ¹¹ For He knew who was going to betray Him, and that was why He said not every one was clean. ¹² When He had finished washing their feet, He put on his clothes and returned to His place. 'Do you understand what I have done for you?' He asked them. ¹³ 'You call Me "Teacher" and "Lord," and rightly so, for that is what I am. ¹⁴ Now that I, your Lord and Teacher, have washed your feet, you also should wash one another's feet. [15] I have set you an example that you should do as I have done for you. [16] Very truly I tell you, no servant is greater than his master, nor is a messenger greater than the one who sent him. [17] Now that you know these things, you will be blessed if you do them.'"

I would have been like Peter and said, "you shall never wash my feet" out of the insecurity of not wanting someone touching mine.

But today, on this date, it's time to wash those feet with Jesus.

We might not see Jesus right in front of us with our physical eyes or feel His physical hands. But may I suggest we take this date to allow Him to symbolically wash our feet? Consider this your time, after having confessed those sins on the prior date, to let Him further wash you. He did this for His disciples, to encourage them to do this for others.

Take a photo of your feet in that bucket, bowl or tub, to commemorate this occasion.

There was a time I did a similar spiritual exercise at the beach. I'll include that photo here. But since this book is trying to help you enjoy times mostly indoors during the fall and winter months, I wanted to make sure you had good options for indoor dates.

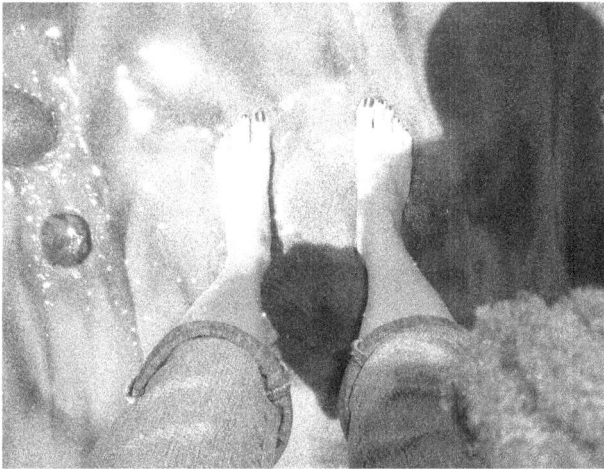

On this intimate date, fill that bucket, bowl or just enough of the tub to put your feet in the warm water. Let them soak. Take a moment before Jesus to be still with Him. Let the salts and the soapy water soak in.

Ask Jesus to make you clean and to prepare you to be His servant. For the next hour, the next day, the next month. This year.

Ask Him to help you be more sensitive to the ways in which He wants you to serve others. He may surprise you. In the moment you are with a friend or family member, He may encourage you to do something for them they won't expect. It may not be washing their literal feet. But after this date, try to keep your ear open to what He may want you to do.

My favorite part of this date is sitting, being

still, resting in the warm water, and waiting on Jesus. I hope you'll enjoy this time of quiet rest as well.

Despite my foot phobia, I hope my ears will be open to hear whatever Jesus wants me to do.

Even if it's to wash someone else's feet.

Date 4
Time with the Potter

Location: A pottery maker's studio, or a store where you can paint pottery, or an online website

Supplies: Internet connection (if you choose the online version)

Reading: Read chapter before your date (unless opting for online exercise)

The process of pottery making has always intrigued me. The Bible talks about pottery as a symbol. And seeing *how* pottery is made into the beautiful pieces they become, I can see why it's a great metaphor. I've used characters as potters in screenplays and a children's book series, *Potter Knows Best*, because of this metaphor.

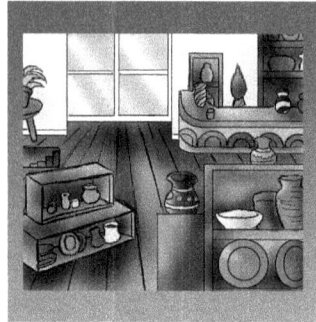

Consider these verses:

"You turn things upside down, as if the potter were thought to be like the clay! Shall what is formed say to the one who formed it, 'You did not make me'? Can the pot say to the potter, 'You know nothing?'" (Isaiah 29:16)

"But the pot he was shaping from the clay was marred in his hands; so the potter formed it into another pot, shaping it as seemed best to him." (Jeremiah 18:4)

"Does not the potter have the right to make out of the same lump of clay some pottery for special purposes and some for common use?" (Romans 9:21)

Even just in those three verses, there are lessons about who's in charge. The maker or the pot. If something goes wrong, can that same piece be repurposed into something else? And can the potter make things for different purposes? So rich with concepts worth pondering.

When I think of God as our Potter, one who is constantly shaping us to be more like Christ, I feel so encouraged. This is because throughout our lives, our purposes can grow and change or morph into something new. I feel like God is right beside us, ready to help move us to the next thing. He can always use us too. I find this really important for my self-esteem, for reminding me that God has a plan. Even if I mess up that plan, He can rearrange things and give me a new purpose.

For today's date, I'm giving an Internet option just in case you do not feel there is a place close enough to home to go to. But before you choose that, try to find a local studio to visit.

My number one suggestion for this date is to go meet a real potter and watch him or her in action. The "throwing pots live in front of you" kind of potter, on the spinning wheel, a place with kilns. See how it works to fashion something from that powdery clay to something beautiful like a plate or vase. (If you want to and can afford it, take classes and become the potter yourself. But you certainly don't need to, to get something out of this date.)

My husband knew I was working on the story for *Potter Knows Best* and that it had been my desire to see a potter in action. To surprise me on our honeymoon, he arranged for a visit to a potter's studio in an adorable small town. I loved it. We got to watch the potter throw pots and expertly shape them the way he wanted them. He had an attached shop where we purchased a vase, which still to this day holds a bouquet we dried from my wedding, our wedding cake topper, and butterflies from the flower bouquet Chris gave me the week he proposed.

Try to visit one of these places. Think through those verses. And then consider all the steps that clay goes through to become what the potter intended.

Then I want you to think about yourself and our Lord. In what ways has He been shaping and molding you into who He wants you to be?

The Word is clear. God wants to shape us to be like Jesus, His Son. This exercise is to help you understand what you were created for, get to know the One who has shaped you deeper, and to recognize all the gifts and purposes He's commissioned over your life.

One of the less desirable processes in our life is to go through fire. But one reason I'd like you to visit a real pottery shop is to notice how much fire and heat plays a role in bringing about the purposes of those pieces. Without fire, they wouldn't be strong. They wouldn't have their dull glazes turned into beautiful colors. Fire takes care of that as well.

After spending some time observing this process and all the steps, I encourage you to take time with the Lord to ask for insights into what ways He's molding and shaping you to be more like Jesus. Then ask for what purposes He wants to use you. Every process we go through can be a divine shaping if we let it.

This process reminds me of a quote I wrote for the movie, *The Ultimate Gift*. It's one of the most often quoted moments from that film that I see posted online. James Garner's character, Red Stevens, tells his grandson on video, "Every process worth going through will get tougher before it gets easier. That's what makes learning a gift, even if pain is your teacher." I wrote that line after being inspired by the process of pottery.

Naturally, we won't be used as literal plates or vases. But I'm sure you can translate this into your life and the ways God may want to use you.

An alternative to a pottery shop is to visit one of those places like Color Me Mine to paint a piece with glaze. Recently, my church's women's group went to a local one in Georgia and spent a fun night out painting. Everyone chose a different piece. You can do this with a group or alone. While there, see if you can get the shop owners to show you their process a bit, like checking out their kiln.

We picked out four colors of glaze to use on each piece. The colors start off looking dull. They have to go through the fire before the colors pop. While there, look at their before and after pieces, to see how dull glazes become pretty once fired. When we picked up our pieces later, they were shiny and beautiful.

For my piece, I chose an ornament that says JOY. Joy had been a theme word of mine for the year and I thought it was most appropriate. I also chose colors like pink, purple, blue, and grey instead of painting it with Christmas colors. I wanted to see this ornament year round.

The last version of this date, if you can't find a local potter or painting shop, is to find an article online by looking up a phrase like "Pottery Making Steps." You can read an article with pictures or even watch a video of a potter to get the same understanding. Then ponder with God how and what He's shaping you into and which pottery making phase you may currently be in.

Finally, no matter which method you chose, think through what it means to be more like Jesus. If that is who our Father God wants to shape us into, what does He mean by that?

Ponder these verses:

"Therefore, I urge you, brothers and sisters, in view of God's mercy, to offer your bodies as a living sacrifice, holy and pleasing to God—this is your true and proper worship. Do not conform to the pattern of this world, but be transformed by the renewing of your mind. Then you will be able to test and approve what God's will is — His good, pleasing and perfect will." (Romans 12:1-2)

"For we are God's handiwork, created in Christ Jesus to do good works, which God prepared in advance for us to do." (Ephesians 2:10)

"...being confident of this, that He who began a good work in you will carry it on to completion until the day of Christ Jesus." (Philippians 1:6)

"For those God foreknew He also predestined to be conformed to the image of his Son, that He might be the firstborn among many brothers and sisters." (Romans 8:29)

God has a purpose for each of us. He shapes us into who He needs us to be and to be more like Christ, especially if we let Him. Trust yourself in the hand of the Potter today.

Date 5
Retreat with Jesus

Location: A retreat center or mission

Supplies: A journal, Bible, praise and worship songs printed or in songbooks, music player, adult coloring books or any other "spiritual" hobby you may have

Reading: Read chapter before and during your date

This date will take planning ahead and a budget. So read the first half of this chapter to find out what it will entail and how to prepare for it. The second part of the chapter includes exercises to do during your spiritual retreat with Jesus.

There's just something about getting away that helps us focus on Jesus.

If you are married, you probably enjoy trips

away with your spouse when you can leave the world behind and spend time having fun together.

This is the same. This will be a long date, on a weekend with Jesus alone, on a private retreat.

In California, there was no shortage of retreat centers where you could get reasonably priced rooms for one or two nights. Some of these were on the properties of missions. I took two retreats at the Mission San Luis Rey in Oceanside, CA, usually getting a room for less than $100 a night. I could bring my own food or pay extra to eat during meals they were serving the staff. These rooms are appropriate too, because they aren't going to be equipped with televisions and other distractions.

Try at the very least to go for one night. But if possible take a long weekend and stay for two. I chose a time when the retreat center wasn't having big groups so the location would be quieter and I'd have better choices to enjoy the secluded places on campus.

I chose places that had chapels or a mission or church building. I chose one with gardens, stations of the cross, walking paths, places to sit by fountains or flowers. I wanted a place with a good variety of spots so I could change my environment when desired. I grew to adore birds at one of these places. They had a fountain that served as a birdbath to many winged creatures. Just watching God's creative design at work was such a joy.

Before your trip, pack clothes, food, supplies you may want, like your Bible, journal, this book, any artistic hobbies you have that you can do while there (like drawing, painting, adult coloring books). Bring an MP3 player or iPad or a way to play music. Bring songbooks or printed lyrics for praise songs, a musical instrument if you play one. Bring comfortable clothes if you want to dance. Pack anything that will help you stay focused on Jesus during this time away.

I suggest leaving your laptop at home, unless you use it as a Bible study tool or for journaling. But try to make this mostly electronics-free if you can. (Except to take photos with your phone or play worship music.)

When I took my trip to Oceanside, I spent most of my time on the retreat center campus. But I did take one field trip to the beach and pier to enjoy a walk with Jesus by the water. So it may help to check out the area you choose to see if there is anything else you may enjoy in the area. (My "feet on the beach" shot was taken during that retreat in Oceanside by the pier.)

At the Retreat

During your retreat, be sensitive to anything Jesus wants to do with you. It's not to be an overly programmed time. You have enough of that in your daily life.

This is a time for rest. Take time to breathe, enjoy the quiet. (There are some retreats you can even ask for a label to wear that says "silent retreat" if you want other people to know not to talk to you. But I never opted for that, as I wanted to sing praise songs and pray out loud.)

At first, it can feel a bit lonely. Especially if you choose a time to do this in life when you're dealing with something difficult like I was the first time I took one. But trust me. You will feel so refreshed by the end.

During the day, I'd enjoy the gardens. The walk through the stations of the cross. Sitting at fountains and journaling or just walking down pathways.

I'll share a few of the photos I took to commemorate my time with Jesus.

I'd also spend time in chapels or sanctuaries the campuses had to offer:

Also, if you get tired during the day, don't be afraid to take a quick nap.

"He will not let your foot slip—He who
watches over you will not slumber." (Psalm
121:3)

"When you lie down, you will not be afraid;
when you lie down, your sleep will be
sweet." (Proverbs 3:24)

At night, I found places to go inside the
buildings, like cozy sitting rooms. I also found a
room that had a piano. Even though I can't play
well, I used that room to sing, dance, or just play
music on my tablet. I only went back to my room
late in the evening since I knew I'd be in there the
rest of the night. But even the room was a quiet
haven.

I took one of my retreats during a season when I was in a lot of emotional pain. I wasn't married yet and had hopes about the love story part of my life finally moving forward. But I had suffered another disappointment. I needed that time away to refocus myself on Jesus. The true Lover of my Soul.

I left far more peaceful than I arrived. And that's what a retreat should be like. However, don't feel like you can only take this retreat when you desperately need it. You can also choose to go out of love, just to spend time with Jesus without distraction. A married couple doesn't just take trips away because their marriage is in trouble. It can also be for fun and focused reconnection.

Even if you are married, you can consider taking a retreat like this with your spouse. (Chris and I returned to the same mission for a two-night stay.) You also can allow each spouse to take a retreat alone. I know one married couple who regularly gives each other the chance to take retreats alone, by shouldering the home responsibilities with their children while the other one is gone. It's hard and a sacrifice, both financially and to have the other spouse gone. But they see such fruit from giving each other this time, this space and grace. They know this is healthy for their marriage and their spiritual life. They aim for at least once a year, if not more. I think it's a worthy investment.

I promise you'll be thankful you have invested

in this time in taking a retreat with Jesus. Don't forget to take some selfies to commemorate for your *Dates With God* scrapbook.

I'll leave you with a couple of last photos from a few of my retreats with Jesus. I hope you will enjoy your time away with Him as much as I did.

Date 6
The Art Gallery

Location: An art gallery or a church known for its stained glass windows

Supplies: None

Reading: Read whole chapter before your date

When I lived in California, one of my favorite nights of the year was "Art Night Pasadena." They'd open up many museums for a Friday night in March and October, provide a shuttle service between 10-15 artistic locations, and let you in for free. There's a similar event sponsored annually by Smithsonian Magazine called Museum Day that happens in many states. During the most recent one, we visited The Martha Berry Museum on the campus of Berry College in Rome, Georgia.

In Pasadena, my favorite location was the Norton Simon Museum. They always had a wing of artwork showing biblical scenes on display.

My encouragement to you is to find a museum that has a display that is of a biblical nature, or an historic church that has gorgeous displays of art on stained glass or murals.

There used to be a historic church in Uptown Charlotte that had a wonderful mural depicting the life of Peter. It has since fallen apart and been painted over. But that's another type of idea, where you could choose to spend this date. Find a church that has artwork about Jesus.

Enjoy some time alone with our Lord, behold the beauty of the creations God has inspired other artists to render. Ponder the scenes displayed, and if desired, look up the Scriptures depicted in those pictures.

In Virginia Beach, while at Regent University, we'd shoot our films at some of the most beautiful historic churches. They sure knew how to create art. Touring those would make a wonderful date.

Of course if you ever find yourself somewhere that you can go to one of the bigger, overtly religious places, do so. (Ex. the Bible Museum.) But for this date, keep it simple and find somewhere local to you.

If you are in California, find some of those missions I mentioned in the retreat chapter.

So, this date is simple to set up. Look up museums or historical cathedrals in your area, and set off to visit them.

Try to get a few selfies of you on this date to add to your *Dates With God* scrapbook later, in front of cathedrals or the museum. (They probably won't let you take pictures with the artwork, especially with a flash, which can fade artwork.)

I hope you enjoy a quiet stroll with Jesus as you behold the works of His creations.

> "You have many workers: stonecutters, masons and carpenters, as well as those skilled in every kind of work in gold and silver, bronze and iron—craftsmen beyond number. Now begin the work, and the LORD be with you." (1 Chronicles 22:15-16)

Date 7
The Encourager

Location: A quiet place at home
Supplies: A phone with texting (or email, if you prefer)
Reading: Read whole chapter during your date

*I*n each installment, I try to pick at least one date that involves serving others. This one is easy but can make a big difference in the life of someone you love or care for. And you don't even have to leave home.

This is one of those service dates that is squarely within my comfort zone.

I got the idea one night when we had an unusually gorgeous night in August that wasn't swelteringly hot. A bonus was the shining moon above. I was able to sit outside on our patio and enjoy the silence of the night, other than the sounds of nature, wind, and crickets.

I sat in that "be still" mode for about thirty minutes. Then, I felt an inspiration from the Lord to do an exercise to encourage others. He is such an encourager of us when we feel down and need it.

> "But you, LORD, are a shield around me, my glory, the One who lifts my head high." (Psalm 3:3)

> "But He said to me, 'My grace is sufficient for you, for my power is made perfect in weakness.' Therefore I will boast all the more gladly about my weaknesses, so that Christ's power may rest on me. That is why, for Christ's sake, I delight in weaknesses, in insults, in hardships, in persecutions, in difficulties. For when I am weak, then I am strong." (2 Corinthians 12:9-10)

I pondered our Lord as our Encourager. I felt like I should pass that along, acting as His hands and feet and even His mouthpiece to encourage others. Have you ever had anyone contact you at just the right time with just the right words you needed to hear?

I wanted to put this into practice for the sake of

others on that night, on my back patio.

But how? And who?

Well, those answers came through sitting there with Jesus in prayer. I asked Jesus if anyone could use encouragement from Him that particular night. It could be through a verse or even a phrase I felt led to type out. The point is it came through praying over whom to text and what to say. I didn't just randomly pick people or choose on my own what to say. I asked Jesus and then I waited.

I felt like Jesus wanted me to send texts to five different friends that night, some of whom I hadn't talked to or checked in with in a while. Again, I let Him lead what I was to say. Honestly, even in sending a verse or a phrase to someone, I may not personally know why I was sending it. I had to send it in faith that it would somehow encourage the receiver.

And it did. I got wonderful responses from people who might have been having a bad night. It may have come through at the right time.

I love when something as simple as this could be a blessing to those people in my life who needed encouragement.

On this date, I suggest you do the same.

Take this date to sit with Jesus, ask who to write to and what to say. Don't make this up from your own reasoning. Ask Him. Let Him lead. Get your Bible out and ask Him to highlight the right verse.

Or even if it's not a Bible verse, ask Him to give you the right words. Then be obedient and send it.

The Word reminds us in Psalm 34:18: "The Lord is close to the brokenhearted and saves those who are crushed in spirit."

Every person you write to may not be on the brink of a breakdown. But I have sent a letter before to someone who said my letter arrived just in time when they were suicidal. You just never know why God may be prompting you to reach out to someone in need. But do so gladly, being His hands, His feet, offering His words of encouragement in their time of need. (You can send actual cards rather than texts if you'd like to, for this date. People don't get mail often today, and it will stand out.)

There is such fulfillment when we can be of service when Jesus is directing us to help someone else. If anyone knows what encouragement someone needs in that exact moment, it's Him.

Just listen, write, and send.

Date 8
Communion with Jesus

Location: At quiet place at home

Supplies: Grape juice, piece of bread, Internet and web browser

Reading: Read chapter during your date

$\mathcal{T}$he Last Supper is one of my favorite scenes to see depicted in artwork, to see Jesus among His best friends, sitting at that long table about to break bread with them.

Jesus wanted them to have a way to remember Him. "And He took bread, gave thanks and broke it, and gave it to them, saying, 'This is my body given for you; do this in remembrance of me'" (Luke

22:19).

Meditate on this Scripture passage from 1 Corinthians 11:23-32:

> "For I received from the Lord what I also passed on to you: The Lord Jesus, on the night He was betrayed, took bread, 24 and when He had given thanks, He broke it and said, 'This is my body, which is for you; do this in remembrance of Me.' 25 In the same way, after supper He took the cup, saying, 'This cup is the new covenant in my blood; do this, whenever you drink it, in remembrance of Me.' 26 For whenever you eat this bread and drink this cup, you proclaim the Lord's death until He comes.
>
> 27 So then, whoever eats the bread or drinks the cup of the Lord in an unworthy manner will be guilty of sinning against the body and blood of the Lord. 28 Everyone ought to examine themselves before they eat of the bread and drink from the cup. 29 For those who eat and drink without discerning the body of Christ eat and drink judgment on themselves. 30 That is why many among you are weak and sick, and a number of you have fallen asleep. 31 But if we were more discerning with regard to ourselves, we would not come under such judgment.

[32] Nevertheless, when we are judged in this way by the Lord, we are being disciplined so that we will not be finally condemned with the world."

Use this opportunity to take time to pray. Have a time of confession, asking the Lord to bring anything to mind you should ask forgiveness for. My husband likes to call this "keeping short accounts." I know you already had that time of confession by the fire pit. But you know how we are. We're human. We still fail at times. Confession is not a one-time thing. And now is a great time to ask forgiveness for anything current.

Then, consider taking a few moments to praise Jesus for His sacrifice on the cross. For His offer of forgiveness and redemption. Then take time to partake of the communion before you. The bread and the juice representing the body and the blood.

Communion is an act of intimacy with Jesus, the Savior of your soul.

End this date by opening your web browser and looking up images from artwork that depicts The Last Supper. A quick search will yield some gorgeous artwork of Jesus with His friends. Imagine yourself sitting there with Him, breaking bread together. Know that He wants to be a constant part of your life. Even if you don't see Him in His physical form like these pictures, know that He desires communion with you every day.

Date 9
To Face the "Fear Not"

Location: To be determined

Supplies: To be determined

Reading: Read chapter before (and during) your date

$\mathcal{H}$ave you seen that social media post that often gets shared, saying that "Fear Not" is in the Bible 365 times? That's equivalent to one reminder per day.

God must have known we would need lots of encouragement about fear to mention it so often in His Word.

For this date, you will determine the time, place, and activity. But the rule is: choose something you have wanted to do but have been too afraid to do. Then face that fear with Jesus (assuming this is a fear you feel He would want you to face).

For some with social anxieties, this could be getting out for social events. ("Scary" Singles Social anyone?) When I was single, I used to be afraid to go to those. Actually, any social events would make me nervous. Most of the time I would rather stay home. Sometimes, the moment I'd arrive at an event, all I wanted to do was head back home.

How about auditioning to be part of your church's drama troupe so you can lend your talents to acting in skits (or church videos)?

Or recording that hidden singing talent and putting that song out on YouTube?

Do you have a talent you've been afraid to use or show people? A gift the Lord has given you that you haven't been using?

Is there something you avoid but feel like you should do, like striking up a conversation with a visitor at a soup kitchen?

Is there a place you have avoided but feel like you should go to? I don't mean dangerous and I'm not even talking about some thrill seeking adventure like skydiving. Instead, think of something that perhaps you should be able to do or even want to be able to do, but fear holds you back. What is that one thing you don't want to be afraid of anymore?

Is there someone you haven't talked to in a long

time, out of fear, that you feel like you should make amends with or reconnect with?

Only you can answer these questions and come up with the most appropriate activity for this date.

Choose that activity and ask Jesus how to plan for it. What do you need, and how will you pull it off? What resources and supplies? Do you need to bring a friend? If so, don't hesitate to ask. But at the same time, it can also be good to face a fear with Jesus alone.

Before you go, immerse yourself in encouraging scriptures that speak to anxiety, worry, and fear.

I'll paste the ones I read often, divided by topic. Read all of them during your date.

ANXIETY/WORRY

When anxiety was great within me, Your consolation brought me joy. (Psalm 94:19)

Anxiety weighs down the heart, but a kind word cheers it up. (Proverbs 12:25)

What do people get for all the toil and anxious striving with which they labor under the sun? (Ecclesiastes 2:22)

So then, banish anxiety from your heart and cast off the troubles of your body... (Ecclesiastes 11:10a)

Therefore I tell you, do not worry about your life, what you will eat or drink; or about your body, what you will wear. Is not life more important than food, and the body more important than clothes? (Matthew 6:25)

Therefore do not worry about tomorrow, for tomorrow will worry about itself... (Matthew 6:34a)

Do not be anxious about anything, but in everything, by prayer and petition, with thanksgiving, present your requests to God. And the peace of God, which transcends all understanding, will guard your hearts and your minds in Christ Jesus." (Philippians 4:6-7)

Cast all your anxiety on Him because He cares for you. (1 Peter 5:7)

FEAR

Even though I walk through the darkest valley, I will fear no evil, for You are with me; Your rod and Your staff, they comfort me. (Psalm 23:4)

The LORD is my light and my salvation—whom shall

I fear? The LORD is the stronghold of my life—of whom shall I be afraid? (Psalm 27:1)

Though an army besiege me, my heart will not fear; though war break out against me, even then will I be confident. (Psalm 27:3)

But whoever listens to me will live in safety and be at ease, without fear of harm. (Proverbs 1:33)

So do not fear, for I am with you; do not be dismayed, for I am your God. I will strengthen you and help you; I will uphold you with My righteous right hand. (Isaiah 41:10)

For I am the LORD your God who takes hold of your right hand and says to you, Do not fear; I will help you. (Isaiah 41:13)

Do not fear, for I have redeemed you; I have summoned you by name; you are Mine. (Isaiah 43:1b)

Do not be afraid; you will not be put to shame. Do not fear disgrace; you will not be humiliated... (Isaiah 54:4a)

You will have nothing to fear. Terror will be far removed; it will not come near you. (Isaiah 54:14b)

But I will rescue you on that day, declares the LORD;

you will not be given into the hands of those you fear. (Jeremiah 39:17)

And my Spirit remains among you. Do not fear. (Haggai 2:5b)

"For God hath not given us the spirit of fear; but of power, and of love, and of a sound mind." (2 Timothy 1:7, kjv)

There is no fear in love. But perfect love drives out fear, because fear has to do with punishment. The one who fears is not made perfect in love. (1 John 4:18)

TRUST

Those who know your name trust in you, for you, LORD, have never forsaken those who seek you. (Psalm 9:10)

Some trust in chariots and some in horses, but we trust in the name of the LORD our God. (Psalm 20:7)

In you our ancestors put their trust; they trusted and you delivered them. (Psalm 22:4)

I trust in you; do not let me be put to shame, nor let

my enemies triumph over me. (Psalm 25:2)

But I trust in you, LORD; I say, "You are my God." (Psalm 31:14)

In Him our hearts rejoice, for we trust in His holy name. (Psalm 33:21)

Trust in the LORD and do good; dwell in the land and enjoy safe pasture. (Psalm 37:3)

Commit your way to the LORD; trust in Him... (Psalm 37:5a)

I trust in God's unfailing love forever and ever. (Psalm 52:8b)

When I am afraid, I put my trust in you. (Psalm 56:3)

In God I trust and am not afraid. What can man do to me? (Psalm 56:11)

Trust in Him at all times, you people; pour out your hearts to Him, for God is our refuge. (Psalm 62:8)

I will say of the LORD, "He is my refuge and my fortress, my God, in whom I trust." (Psalm 91:2)

You who fear Him, trust in the LORD—He is their help and shield. (Psalm 115:11)

Let the morning bring me word of your unfailing love, for I have put my trust in you. Show me the way I should go, for to you I entrust my life. (Psalm 143:8)

Trust in the LORD with all your heart and lean not on your own understanding; in all your ways submit to Him, and He will make your paths straight. (Proverbs 3:5–6)

Fear of man will prove to be a snare, but whoever trusts in the LORD is kept safe. (Proverbs 29:25)

Surely God is my salvation; I will trust and not be afraid. The LORD, the LORD Himself is my strength and my defense; He has become my salvation. (Isaiah 12:2)

Trust in the LORD forever, for the LORD, the LORD Himself, is the Rock eternal. (Isaiah 26:4)

"I will save you; you will not fall by the sword but will escape with your life, because you trust in Me," declares the LORD. (Jeremiah 39:18)

The LORD is good, a refuge in times of trouble. He cares for those who trust in Him. (Nahum 1:7)

Now that you have immersed yourself in the truth from God's Word, go without fear into the adventure with Jesus that you have chosen.

Date 10
A Novel Idea

Location: A quiet place at home
Supplies: A novel
Reading: Read chapter before your date

Sometimes, it's pleasant to have a cozy date inside, isn't it? This is a great winter or rainy day activity. It will likely extend over the course of a few dates, unless you're a speed-reader. (I most definitely am not!)

Use this time to prep for the date.

I love stories. I was born to tell them. Sometimes, I like to read nonfiction works to help me when I'm going through something specific. But other times, I like to settle into a good novel. One with good drama and conflict and even those that mirror some of the challenges I'm facing in my real life.

That's what this date (or dates) is going to be about. This isn't about a fictional escape from reality. I'd like you to find a novel, from the Christian fiction genre, to read. Find one where the heroine of the story is experiencing a challenge or trial that you currently face in your life. One that you could use a listening ear for, an understanding heart, a "friend" who already understands the emotions you are dealing with.

Then read the novel, not only for the fictional entertainment value, but also as one that gives you a chance to journey with a character to whom you relate.

It can be cathartic to dive into the world of someone else experiencing the same emotions you are, even if that world is fictional.

I can speak from experience: novelists often write "fiction" works that are not entirely fictional. We give our characters challenges that we have personally experienced (or are still experiencing) because we feel like we can share from a place of understanding.

If you find an author's book that mimics your current life experience, you may learn different ways to handle a similar problem. You may just feel like you have a friend who understands you. I also suggest as you embark on reading whatever novel you choose, you welcome God to speak to you through this book. I can't tell you how much it means to me when I hear from readers about how relatable my characters are. I often hear how my books help them with a particular struggle that I know all too well I relate to. (I usually write stories I relate to on some emotional level.)

Pinpoint an issue you'd like to read a book about. Do a search for Christian Fiction books on that topic and see what you come up with. Make sure it's well reviewed.

Author Katie Ganshert has shared publicly about her struggles with infertility and gave that challenge to her character in *The Art of Losing Yourself.* Also in *Wildflowers in Winter*, Ganshert offers a fantastic read for those dealing with loss of a spouse and infertility. Then in its sequel, *Wishing on Willows*, it shows the continuation of that story as the character struggles to move forward in life after loss. (If you follow Katie's true-life journey to parenthood and adoption, you can understand why these themes end up in more than one of her novels.)

For those who need guidance with a rebellious child, *The Prayer Box* by Lisa Wingate is good.

Karen Kingsbury's novel, *On Every Side*, deals with anger after loss. Kingsbury's book *Unlocked* is a wonderful example of growing to understand a special needs young man, who has autism.

Susan Rohrer's *Gifted* also tackles taking care of a special needs sibling, while her novel *Grace Dawns* will resonate with those taking care of aging parents.

For those struggling with being bullied themselves or with their children being bullied, read *Listen* by Rene Gutteridge. Gutteridge's book *Just 18 Summers* (with Michelle Cox) deals with parenting at various stages of life.

To put a plug in for a couple of my own novels, *Never the Bride* (co-authored with Gutteridge) contains the theme of facing singlehood. It's about trusting in God's plan, no matter how long God waits to write that love story.

My novel *Song of Springhill* deals with a crisis of faith and what my lead character is to believe about a God who allows bad things to happen. It's inspired by actual mining disasters.

Naturally, the choices out there will be endless. You just need to narrow your search to a journey you'd like to experience through a fictional character. Take time on these dates to read the novel, then ask God to help you learn and even heal through the journey of the character you chose to read about.

I know for me, writing about my extremely long singlehood journey through *Never the Bride* did a lot for my relationship with God.

Jesus often used parables and stories with symbols to speak, rather than overtly preaching. He wanted His listeners to take time to think about things, to bring up questions based on these parables. There are over 30 of them in the Bible.

I'll just share one example here. *The Parable of the Lost Sheep* from Luke 15:1-7:

> "Now the tax collectors and sinners were all gathering around to hear Jesus. 2 But the Pharisees and the teachers of the law muttered, 'This man welcomes sinners and eats with them.' 3 Then Jesus told them this parable: 4 'Suppose one of you has a hundred sheep and loses one of them. Doesn't he leave the ninety-nine in the open country and go after the lost sheep until he finds it? 5 And when he finds it, he joyfully puts it on his shoulders 6 and goes home. Then he calls his friends and neighbors together and says, "Rejoice with me; I have found my lost sheep." 7 'I tell you that in the same way there will be more rejoicing in heaven over one sinner who repents than over ninety-nine righteous persons who do not need to repent.'"

At the end of the parable, in this case, Jesus lets the listeners know what He's talking about. Not sheep, but sinners. Whether those who heard the story would translate this to their own lives is up to them. Not everyone believed they were lost back then, which of course is a lot like many people today who don't believe they need a Savior. Bethel Worship has a song based on this parable called *Reckless Love*, its own version of retelling this story.

Stories are powerful, whether in a song, in a novel, in the Bible, or even in movies or on TV. Use this date (or series of dates) by diving into the story of a fictional character facing something you are also facing in your life, to let God speak to you.

Let Jesus minister to you through story, just like He so often did through parables in His Word.

Date 11
Stations of the Cross

Location: A mission or location, which hosts The Stations of the Cross. Alternative: a website that has artwork and descriptions for each of them.

Supplies: None (unless you opt for Internet version)

Reading: Read chapter before your date

Living in California, there were a good amount of locations that hosted The Stations of the Cross. It was my first introduction to these types of meditation places when on dates with God.

I want to encourage you to take a date with Jesus like this.

First, look up the phrase "The Stations of the

Cross" and your city and state. See what comes up in a search. See if there is one local enough to visit. (Preferably in the fall or spring when it's not too cold.) Just doing a search for Georgia, I found them anywhere from Atlanta to Athens to Savannah. They were at churches of various denominations, and retreat centers. In California they were often at missions. But if there isn't one close enough to you, I'll pose an alternative online date.

Because this book focuses on dates specifically with Jesus, I wanted to honor Him by highlighting the Stations of the Cross and give you a date to focus on each phase of His divine story.

(Example, Station 2: Jesus accepts His cross)

Normally, in a garden or somewhere outside on a church property, they'll walk you through 14 stations. Each one covers a different part of Jesus' story on His way to the cross. Walking through each station can be a meaningful time for reflection of Jesus' loving sacrifice on our behalf. Many locations have artwork to behold as you focus on each one separately.

Here are the names of the stations often depicted by these special gardens or tributes to Jesus on church properties:

1. Pilate condemns Jesus to die
2. Jesus accepts His cross
3. Jesus falls for the first time
4. Jesus meets His mother, Mary
5. Simon of Cyrene helps carry the cross
6. Veronica wipes the face of Jesus (from Catholic tradition, not recorded in Scripture.)
7. Jesus falls for the second time
8. Jesus meets the women of Jerusalem
9. Jesus falls for the third time
10. Jesus is stripped of His clothes
11. Jesus is nailed to the cross
12. Jesus dies on the cross

13. Jesus is taken down from the cross

14. Jesus is placed in the tomb

Only limited displays show a fifteenth step: Jesus' resurrection. Naturally, I choose to honor that moment as well, regardless of whether the stations do or not.

Each step in the process is worthy of taking your time to walk through, to ponder, to read the Scriptures that go with the steps, if they have them on plaques. (I've visited these displays in Solvang and Oceanside at two of the missions in California.)

It's a great way to honor our Savior for what He did for us on that cross by walking alongside His journey to that cross.

If you can't find one local enough to go to or if the weather is too cold, look up "Stations of the Cross" online. Find prose descriptions of each station as well as images where you will often find a collage of fourteen photos. They will help you walk through each station virtually. Stay in where it's warm, pour a cup of tea, and take time to read and reflect about each one.

Regardless of whether you do this date on the site of a church garden displaying the stations or at home, end this date writing a love note of thanks to Jesus for all He did for you on that cross.

Date 12
Prayer and Fasting

Location: Anywhere
Supplies: TBD
Reading: Read whole chapter before your date

$\mathcal{A}$t the beginning of each year, our church (among many others) moves into a time of prayer and fasting. In our case, they plan 21 days. The first week is earmarked for both prayer and fasting while the next 14 of 21 are for continued prayer. They have a new blogger write a post each day, to keep us encouraged and motivated. They hold prayer meetings over the Internet at a designated time each day.

They let us choose what type of fast to

participate in. The two main suggestions were a liquids-only fast or the Daniel Fast. However, we weren't limited to those two options. Many of the women chose to do a liquids-only fast but with the addition of smoothies. This allowed us to blend our fruits and veggies into liquid form. (Some did this for health reasons, too. Personally, I can't go a day without collagen powder due to leg pain. That eliminates the Daniel Fast, as they don't allow any meat or products derived from animals, like collagen is.) We didn't want to approach the fast in a legalistic way, instead in a way we felt would be healthy and God-led. (Some chose to also fast from media.)

Jesus is our example. He fasted for forty days and nights and spent a lot of time in prayer. He also said there were certain things that had to be prayed through with both prayer and fasting. It was as if sometimes, prayer alone wasn't enough. (See the story in Mark 9:14-29.)

Here are some verses that promote both:

"In the first year of his reign, I, Daniel, understood from the Scriptures, according to the word of the Lord given to Jeremiah the prophet, that the desolation of Jerusalem would last seventy years. So I turned to the Lord God and pleaded with Him in prayer and petition, in fasting, and in sackcloth and ashes. I prayed to the Lord my God and confessed: 'Lord, the great and awesome God, who keeps His covenant of love with those who love Him and keep His commandments.'" (Daniel 9:2-4)

"Paul and Barnabas appointed elders for them in each church and, with prayer and fasting, committed them to the Lord, in whom they had put their trust." (Acts 14:23)

So my encouragement for you is to determine, in prayer with Jesus, what type of prayer and fasting you should commit to.

What does the fasting component look like and how long? What will you eat or not eat? What does the prayer portion look like? What are your goals? What times of day will you pray and for how long?

Write it all down. I found that writing down what was on my "allowed to eat" list held me accountable to it. To be honest, when I didn't make a concerted list of what I hoped to do in prayer, I didn't do as well as I did in following the fasting portion.

Since fasting and times of prayer were so important to Jesus, I feel like they are good keys to intimacy with Him.

What time of year you do this and how often

will be up to you and the Lord. The beginning of the year is always a nice time to kick start something like this. However, it's not an exclusive time. Any time of year can be a time to focus on prayer and fasting. You can even do one day of prayer and fasting per month or per quarter. It doesn't have to be 21 days in January. I enjoyed that for the accountability with church and to be supportive of their initiative. But in the world of *Dates With God*, this is also about our personal spiritual practices.

The important thing is to let Jesus lead. I encourage you to fast even when you don't have a dire prayer issue. Don't always make it about one specific breakthrough you are hoping to obtain or one specific prayer purpose.

Sometimes, a time of prayer and fasting can simply be about getting to know Jesus on a deeper level. Especially when we use those meal times we may be skipping to hang out with Jesus instead. Some of my extra time not spent in the kitchen was spent on casual walks with our Lord. I treasure those moments with Him. And you can too.

Date 13
A Feast with Jesus

Location: Your kitchen
Supplies: A cookbook, supplies to cook a meal
Reading: Read chapter before your date

$\mathcal{A}$ren't dates out to dinner some of your favorites? Almost no one goes on a date and doesn't find themselves either at a coffee shop, ice cream shop, or restaurant. There's something intimate about sharing a meal and conversation together.

In my screenplay and novel for *Never the Bride*, there is a sequence where Jessie invites God over for a date while she cooks her favorite meal for herself. That scene inspired this date.

While I'm not suggesting you literally make a plate for Jesus at your dinner table and serve it, I am suggesting you "make room" for Him at the table.

> "Jesus said to them, 'Come and have
> breakfast.' None of the disciples dared ask
> Him, 'Who are you?' They knew it was the
> Lord. Jesus came, took the bread and gave
> it to them, and did the same with the fish."
> (John 21:12-13)

Some translations of that verse use the phrase, "Come and dine."

My husband and I live in one of those open-concept homes with a large island to cook on. When standing at the kitchen island with my feet one of those cushy, memory foam floor mats, I have a great view of our television. Often when I cook, my favorite thing to do is turn on Netflix or Hulu or Pure Flix and watch a movie or TV show. (I especially like to do this when I do my month-ahead-cooking marathon days. Great for binge watching and helps me not get bored with the chore of hours of cooking.)

To make this a date with Jesus, keep that television off. This is a leisurely time to spend with Jesus while you cook. Take time to chat with Jesus. You can play some light music in the background if you want. Even light candles if you feel like it.

Make a meal, maybe even one that follows some biblical format for eating, like foods from biblical feasts. Or consider a meal incorporating fresh fish and bread, as mentioned in that verse when Jesus asked His disciples to dine with Him. But don't feel obligated to do that. You can prepare something healthy and something you enjoy. (I'm a big fan of cacao powder based desserts. Superfood!) Make it a three or four course meal. (If you have an elderly neighbor, consider making enough to deliver a food care package to them.)

Don't wait until it's time to sit down and eat to interact with Jesus. The idea is to commune with Him during meal preparation too. Pray out loud while you cook.

Then sit with Jesus. Pray over your meal and your time together, and enjoy the courses of your meal. You could even pick a different topic of conversation for each course.

Enjoy talking to Him while you enjoy one of those senses that our Lord Himself gave to us that is an incredible gift: our sense of taste.

As Psalm 34:8 reminds us, "Taste and see that the LORD is good; blessed is the one who takes refuge in Him."

So that's it! This date is simple yet still intimate and meaningful. (And one that is making me hungry. Time for a date.)

Date 14
The Bride of Christ

Location: A quiet place at home
Supplies: A computer, Bible, journal
Reading: Read chapter during your date

The Bride of Christ. A phrase I've heard for many years. It's usually in reference to the church Jesus returns to gather. But what does it mean? Where do we fit into a phrase like that? Will we be ready to be a bride for Jesus?

I won't paste particular Bible references inside this book, since this date is to be enjoyed in your cozy home with a Bible and a computer. I want you to use those tools to look up passages of Scripture and cross-reference sections.

Start by looking up the Parable of the 10 virgins, which is about how to be ready for the return of our bridegroom. (Matthew 25:1-18)

Then, ask Jesus how He sees you as part of this "Bride of Christ" He mentions returning for. Look up any references you can find that talk about the church being The Bride of Christ, and about Jesus being our bridegroom.

Dig deep into all those references and how Jesus talks about Himself and us.

Then think through the following:

What do those passages mean to you?

What do you think about knowing Jesus sees you as His bride?

Does it depend on your sense of love and commitment to Him?

I love that in His Word, He refers to us this way, as His bride. It gives me a sense of belonging.

I want to make sure you come through this date series knowing full well, without a doubt, the deep love that Jesus has for you, His bride, His creation.

If you are married, how did you feel the day you put on that wedding dress and walked toward your groom? I believe our Jesus is no less romantic.

He is waiting, with eyes on us, ready for us to look at Him *and only Him* with the love He's had for us since the beginning of time.

If you're willing, as an extension of this date, try on a wedding dress. If you're already married and still have your old dress, put it on. Or go to Goodwill and try on a used dress, as a symbol of being Christ's special bride.

Date 15
On the Vineyard

Location: A vineyard or winery or fruit tree farm
Supplies: None
Reading: Read whole chapter before your date

$\mathcal{I}$ know. It may seem odd to those who don't drink that I'd suggest a date at a winery. Although, wine making was Jesus' first miracle. But it's not to go wine tasting. It's to take a tour of a place that goes through some of those processes the Word uses as an illustration in my favorite chapter of the Bible.

John 15.

Look for a vineyard close enough to visit.

Alternatively, you could also look for a farm that grows fruit trees. What I'm looking for, for this date, is a place where you can watch a gardener go through the process of pruning or harvesting or any stage of the process that is similar to what Jesus talks about in this chapter.

If you don't have one in your area, similar to the suggestion I made in the pottery chapter, you can research online an article about what grapes and vines go through in the process of bearing fruit. (The same goes for researching what happens on a farm where they grow fruit trees.)

Jesus' words in this chapter are such a vivid picture of how we can grow, including through the pruning process, one we may not always enjoy. But it is highly necessary for our growth.

Whether you decide to visit a winery or tree farm to observe the caretaker's process, or research online, I'd like you first to meditate on John 15:1-17:

> "I am the true vine, and My Father is the Gardener. 2 He cuts off every branch in Me that bears no fruit, while every branch that does bear fruit He prunes so that it will be even more fruitful. 3 You are already clean because of the word I have spoken to you. 4 Remain in Me, as I also remain in you. No branch can bear fruit by itself; it must remain in the vine. Neither can you bear fruit unless you remain in Me. 5 'I am the vine; you are the branches. If you remain in Me and I in

you, you will bear much fruit; apart from Me you can do nothing. 6 If you do not remain in Me, you are like a branch that is thrown away and withers; such branches are picked up, thrown into the fire and burned. 7 If you remain in Me and My words remain in you, ask whatever you wish, and it will be done for you. 8 This is to My Father's glory, that you bear much fruit, showing yourselves to be My disciples.' 9 As the Father has loved Me, so have I loved you. Now remain in My love. 10 If you keep My commands, you will remain in My love, just as I have kept My Father's commands and remain in His love. 11 I have told you this so that My joy may be in you and that your joy may be complete. 12 My command is this: Love each other as I have loved you. 13 Greater love has no one than this: to lay down one's life for one's friends. 14 You are My friends if you do what I command. 15 I no longer call you servants, because a servant does not know his master's business. Instead, I have called you friends, for everything that I learned from My Father I have made known to you. 16 You did not choose Me, but I chose you and appointed you so that you might go and bear fruit—fruit that will last—and so that whatever you ask in My name the Father will give you. 17 This is My command: Love each other."

There is so much rich texture to this chapter, lessons to glean from Jesus' words.

Take the time now to explore the vineyard, and the normal process the caretaker uses for harvesting, crushing or pressing, pruning etc. Ask about the process they use to keep their trees or vines bearing fruit and what happens when they stop bearing fruit. (In different seasons, we took wagon tours of Mercier Orchards in Blue Ridge, Georgia, which was interesting to hear how they do everything, and how those processes change when the fruit changes.)

If you are observing vines, try to look at the vines versus the branches, that Jesus mentions. You'll never read those verses the same way again. And you'll come to a better understanding of what Jesus had in mind when using that process to explain what He does with us to keep us bearing fruit.

For Him.

Then, as the final step of this date, ask Jesus what kind of fruit He'd like to see you bearing over the course of the next week.

You can start with the Fruit of the Spirit:

"But the fruit of the Spirit is love, joy,

peace, forbearance, kindness, goodness, faithfulness, gentleness and self-control. Against such things there is no law." (Galatians 5:22-23)

Date 16
Soaking In Galilee

Location: A quiet, private place

Supplies: Sea of Galilee soaking CD (downloadable for free online), journal and pen

Reading: Read whole chapter before your date

In the nineties, when I was a young but serious believer, I was introduced to a book called *Dialogue With God*. (It's since changed titles many times, as it's had new editions over the years. Its current title is *4 Keys to Hearing God's Voice*. It's written by the Virklers, who run Communion with God Ministries and Christian Leadership University.)

That book and future editions revolutionized my life and my relationship with God. It presented the idea God would speak directly to me in such a clear way, unpacking Scriptures about God's desire to commune with us. Maybe not audibly, but in a way I could discern and write down in a journal. *Two-way dialoguing.*

It changed my life. If you have no idea what I'm talking about, I encourage you to read books by the Virklers that share about hearing God's voice.

Meanwhile, they have made available to us, for free, an amazing resource for our quiet times alone with Jesus, the *Sea of Galilee* MP3. It's a musically based track for about 30 minutes that you can journal to. Most of it is instrumental but some of it walks you through an exercise where you close your eyes, picture yourself with Jesus on the Sea of Galilee. In light of that, it's why I thought this would be a neat exercise to use for a date in this volume, focused on Jesus.

(NOTE: At the time of publication, the necessary tools are available for free online. This is being used by permission of Mark Virkler / Communion with God Ministries for this date. The website is: https://www.cwgministries.org/galilee.)

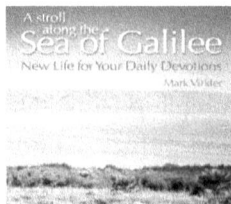

Here are the official instructions they offer for this exercise:

> Pull up this video on your player or listen to it on your iPod during your morning devotional time. Let us paint a scene of you and Jesus walking together along the Sea of Galilee. We'll encourage you to ask Him one of the following questions:
>
> *Lord, what would You like to say to me?*
>
> *How do You see me?*
>
> *Do You love me?*
>
> We then guide you into using the four keys for hearing God's voice, which are: quieting yourself down, fixing your eyes on Jesus, tuning to spontaneity, and writing.
>
> After the 5-minute quieting exercise, where you are taken for a stroll with Jesus along the Sea of Galilee, there follows 25 minutes of anointed music playing softly in the background which is ideal music to journal by (composed by Julie True).
>
> The format of this Stroll Along the Sea of Galilee makes these daily conversations with Jesus easy and effortless. It is designed

to lead you directly and immediately into the experience of hearing God's voice and seeing visions. It also makes an ideal gift to give to your friends to introduce them to experiencing God's voice during their devotional times.

I was at a conference where Mark Virkler personally walked us through a similar exercise. It was so neat to write down what we felt like Jesus was saying and then share that with other attendees.

I hope you enjoy your time on this date, communing with Jesus who loves you so much, who craves to spend this intimate time with you.

Date 17
Painting the Town

Location: At home first, then a small town or bike trail

Supplies: Rocks, paints and brushes or small piece of art to create

Reading: Read whole chapter before your date

$\mathcal{D}$o you like the idea of making a stranger smile? Uplifting someone's day, even if you aren't there to witness it? That's what "painting the town" is about — or painting rocks or art.

In my town, there is an initiative that groups such as the Girl Scouts, clubs, and church groups are taking on. They get together to paint small rocks with pretty drawings or encouraging messages. Then they head into town and hide them for others to find.

You never know when someone might come across your special designs (or rocks). It might brighten their day.

This date comes in two parts. First, you will spend painting your rocks with art or messages. Consider putting short Bible verses on them or Bible phrases or references. As usual, I'm going to encourage you to ask Jesus what to make. (He knows who is going to find it!)

Then you will go out and hide them (at the same time or on a separate date) on bike trails, in planters, in flowerpots around town, or other places you think people may happen upon them.

Our town made it extra fun with participating stores and restaurants hiding some for special giveaways. The stores would post on the town website that they'd hidden some rocks with coupons and give hints on where to find them, turning it into a scavenger hunt. I'm encouraging you to use your rocks with inspiring messages, artwork, or both.

Find out if your town already participates in this. If so, they may have a list of "Take One, Leave One" locations where you can treat it like a scavenger hunt and look for rocks in addition to hiding new ones. If you find one that speaks to you, you can take it home.

Our Visitor's Center holds that list. Just do a little research to find out if a place near you participates. Some hashtags I've seen use the name of the town followed by the word "rocks."

To add to this date, if your town or Visitor's Center also participates in the Little Library program or the Little Pantry program, bring a book you can leave or canned goods or toiletries for the pantry. You will be helping someone in need.

In our town, all three of these opportunities are run through our Visitor's Center. If you find none of them exist nearby, consider starting one of those programs. (If they are in different places, then make these activities separate dates.)

What I love about the idea of hiding these decorative rocks is that your message might just be the one someone needs at the exact moment the Lord leads them to find it, even if they're not looking for it.

Maybe there's even one Jesus wants you to find, for Him to say hello to you or encourage you. It works both ways.

To give you an example of what a rock could say, I saw one that said, "He's my Rock." It had a scripture reference from Psalms. But you can write whatever you feel led to write.

If you don't like painting, an alternative to this style of a date is geocaching. Make caches to hide in old film canisters, hide them, and track your GPS coordinates. Then you post the caches' coordinates on websites for others to find. I've been geocaching before and it's fun. I made ones with a sign-in book so people could let me know if they found it. Inside, I made sure to include some Bible verse cards with encouragement on them.

I also heard of another artistic initiative that some towns participate in called "Free Art Fridays" (or FAF). It's known as an art treasure hunt. Some groups will take that Friday to drop off art in hidden places around town. They ask people to post on social media if they find a piece. It's normally labeled "I'm Free" if it's available to be taken and part of the FAF initiative. They also encourage participants to leave clues online as to where to find them. That would be another fun way to approach this date if your area participates.

Regardless of which activity you choose, enjoy the artistic scavenger hunt with Jesus.

Take pictures of the treasures you find or hide for others. Be sure to spread encouragement through artwork of your own.

Date 18
To Book a Date

Location: A local bookstore or library
Supplies: A journal
Reading: Read chapter before your date

$\mathcal{B}$ookstores are becoming harder to find these days. Thankfully, they still exist. We have charming local versions that are not part of big chains. It's a good thing we still have libraries too. And that is a good alternative to a bookstore for this date if you prefer. Either way, it's another of those you can enjoy during the cooler days of autumn or the chilly days of winter.

Once you choose your location, prepare to spend an hour or two there. Find the section of

Christian books, in this case nonfiction. Choose a
topic you feel you need to read about right now.
Perhaps a book that will encourage you in a trial you
are facing or with an emotional challenge, like fear,
anxiety, breaking addictions, facing life changes, or
loss. It could be a book on how to study the Word, or
go deeper with God or anything else on your heart.

Ask Jesus to pinpoint a book you should take a
look at. Be sensitive to His Spirit or nudge as He
leads.

Choose two to three books off the shelf on this
same topic. They can be nonfiction, self-help, or an
autobiography. I love reading a personal story of
someone facing something I'm dealing with. Or even
those who overcome obstacles I'm not specifically
struggling with but still manage to keep their faith in
tact. (One example for anyone going through a
tough season is Lysa TerKeurst's *It's Not Supposed to
be This Way*.)

Most stores or libraries have cozy areas to sit
and read. So curl up on a comfy chair or couch or at
a small desk, if they have one, and settle in to read
for a bit. Read at least the first chapter of each book
you choose.

If one of them truly speaks to you and you want
to know more, consider buying it or checking it out
of the library. Some libraries have an eBook lending
program too.

One reason I suggest you start reading this book

at the bookstore or library is to get you away from home, your distractions, your usual electronics, and enjoy someone else's quiet, reading environment.

When I was researching children's book writing for *Potter Knows Best*, I enjoyed going to the children's section of my local library, sitting at a table, and reading through many books. (The chairs were a bit short in that area. But it was fun being in an environment meant for children. I found it inspiring.)

This is the same idea, except you will go through the beginnings of books that may speak to a situation you face. Let Jesus sit beside you and speak to you about your life. Perhaps He'll offer a healing balm as you read something you relate to.

Let it be a relaxing time, away from every distraction. Don't be in a hurry. Feel free to also journal your thoughts about what you're reading or journal out a prayer about how you want to grow in this area of life.

Once you complete this date, read the whole book. If you still feel like you want to read more about the issue, find Christian bloggers who speak to the same issue you're facing and comb through their posts. I can't tell you how many times I've found a blogger who sounded like they were getting inside my head (especially during my years of being single and waiting too long for a husband). I always found it cathartic to read other people's emotional journeys, walking through the same things.

May Jesus be with you every step, through books, blogs, and your own prayer journaling to follow.

Date 19
Small Town Tour

Location: A small town, close enough for a day trip from your home

Supplies: A camera

Reading: Read whole chapter before your date

$\mathcal{M}$y husband and I absolutely love taking day trips. We live close to lots of small mountain towns that we can get to and from in one day. While this is outside, I don't suggest waiting for warm weather. In fact, visiting small towns when they are decorated for harvest seasons or Christmas is the most charming part about this date. You may find some Jesus symbols that time of year since Christmas is a celebration of His birth for many of us. (We recently visited Dahlonega, Georgia, for my birthday and it was adorable for Christmas, like being in a Hallmark movie. It was used for an INSP Christmas movie.)

This date is about you and Jesus. Not you and a friend or date or spouse. Pick a small town, drive there, and enjoy your day alone with Jesus.

This is a great date for photos and selfies, so bring your camera or phone to take them.

I love to choose what's known as Main Street Towns that have a quaint town center to start with. In Georgia, there are many of those. But they also happen to be near lots of brooks, rivers, or streams, just to add to the beauty. They offer more places for times of rest with Jesus.

In Helen, Georgia, I enjoy not only the adorable town itself but the swings they place at various points along the Chattahoochee River.

I want you to enjoy a stroll around whatever town you choose. Be on the lookout for what I like to call Godwinks, the term SQuire Rushnell and his wife, Louise Duart, have used in their book series.

Take pictures of anything that reminds you of Jesus. It could be encouraging phrases engraved on benches or interesting license plates. (I wish I could publish the many photos of license plates I've taken, but I have a feeling that would be frowned upon by their owners. One I saw had an acronym that spelled out God's Girl.)

Most small towns have antique shops. Stroll through the booths and see if anything catches your eye. In one store in Riverside, California, I was amazed to see a Christmas village that was just like the one we had when I was a child, complete with a church.

Enjoy taking photos during this date. (And don't forget the selfies!)

When I was on a date with Jesus at a garden in the small town called Arcadia, I enjoyed finding the bench in the following photo, and allowing it to inspire me to sing the Christian hymn that goes with it.

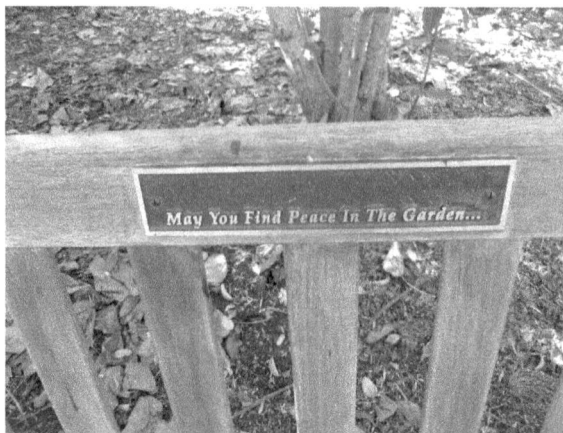

Anything you see that means something to you or to your relationship with Jesus, get a photo. Save these for your scrapbook date to come near the end of this installment of dates.

If an affordable item in an antique store means something to you, buy it. Take it home as a reminder of this date. I did that once with a tiny plaque that had a phrase on it: *The Gift of Love is a Treasure*. I was single and had just written *The Ultimate Gift*.

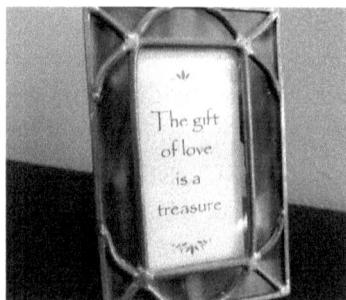

I told God that I felt like I'd experienced all the gifts except love—in a context of a marital relationship. God nudged me to purchase this little plaque, as a reminder He had this gift coming for me in the future.

Go on your own treasure hunt. Find what Jesus will show you today on your adventure in one of these small towns.

Keep those eyes opened and be ready to see.

Date 20
What a Friend We Have in Jesus

Location: A place to enjoy the outdoor activity of your
   choosing
Supplies: TBD
Reading: Read chapter before your date

Remember that old hymn, *What a Friend We Have
in Jesus*? In the 1800s, Joseph Scriven wrote this well-
known hymn:

> What a friend we have in Jesus,
> All our sins and griefs to bear.
> What a privilege to carry
> Everything to God in prayer.
> Oh, what peace we often forfeit;

Oh, what needless pain we bear.
All because we do not carry
Everything to God in prayer.

Have we trials and temptations?
Is there trouble anywhere?
We should never be discouraged.
Take it to the Lord in prayer.
Can we find a friend so faithful
Who with all our sorrows share?
Jesus knows our every weakness.
Take it to the Lord in prayer.

Are we weak and heavy-laden,
Cumbered with a load of care?
Precious Savior, still our refuge.
Take it to the Lord in prayer.
Do your friends despise, forsake you?
Take it to the Lord in prayer.
In His arms He'll take and shield you;
You will find a solace there.

I love the idea of thinking of Jesus as a friend. Not just our Savior or our Brother.

A Friend.

Just like it says in John 15:15, "I no longer call you servants, because a servant does not know his master's business. Instead, I have called you friends, for everything that I learned from my Father I have made known to you."

Today is about friendship. And friends like to do fun activities together, don't they?

My pastor recently preached a sermon, inspired by a message by Craig Groeschel, on true friendship. He talked about how we all need strong friends in our lives. Those strong friends should represent some of the best friends represented in the Bible: Samuel, Jonathan, and Nathan.

Think of Samuel as the friend who sees you for who you can be (seeing David as a future king when he was just a small, shepherd boy.) Think of Jonathan, the friend who wasn't jealous of the position of David. As the son of a King, Jonathan should have been in line for that position. Instead, Jonathan wanted what was best for David and was a faithful and supportive friend. This included being protective of David when Jonathan's own father wanted to kill him. Think of a friend like Nathan, one who's willing to call you out on your messes and try to encourage you to be a better person.

Can you think through the ways in which Jesus personifies these three types of friends to you?

One who sees the best in you, encourages you to be your best, and move toward your calling.

One who supports you and protects you in

that calling.

One who encourages you to do better in areas you feel weak.

This most supportive friend can also be a whole lot of fun to hang out with. And that's what you're going to do on this date.

During this date, I'd love for your thoughts to ponder all the ways in which Jesus embodies these three types of friends to you.

This will likely be a date you will need to get outside. So bundle up. Or plan this one during the fall when it's still nice enough out to be outside. Maybe even when the autumn leaves are at their peak so you can enjoy the beauty of God's creation that way.

What is your favorite outdoor activity?

Two of mine include bike riding down the Georgia trail systems (the ones meant for bikers and walkers, away from traffic) and disc golf, with real discs and not cheapie lightweight ones.

Both of these activities tend to be in the most gorgeous places with lots of trees and nature trails. If you haven't tried disc golf, it's a lot of fun with many options to go to that are often free. Some state parks have courses too. They tend to be anywhere from 9-18 holes. Approach these activities as a fun date with Jesus and no other agenda. Just get some time alone with Him. It's especially fun in the fall if you can enjoy some beautiful places.

Additionally, in my neighborhood for a quick and close-by date, we have tennis courts (one with a small wall to hit balls against) and basketball courts. They aren't used often so I can go by myself and get some time alone, shooting hoops or hitting a tennis ball against that hard wall.

I usually set some kind of "game of one" goal, like spelling three words, where I get a letter for each basket. On this type of date, I'll choose biblical words, like fruits of the Spirit. I'll shoot baskets until I successfully spell as many fruits as I feel like spelling out. (Ex. Joy, peace, patience, kindness.)

Just make sure you enjoy the activity. Don't make it about heavy prayer time. Just enjoy each other's company. This also gets you away from the computer, the distractions of real life, and out for some fresh air!

We have a kayak and I think it would be a blast to do that with Jesus. But so far, only my husband knows how to set our kayak up (and it's hard for me to carry alone since it's a tandem kayak). So I haven't done that alone just yet. But there's something romantic about the idea of setting off on the lakes around here, surrounded by mountains that could be a fun time with Jesus. But only do that if you know how and feel like that's safe to do and if you can manage your kayak alone. Personally, I wouldn't do that. But for some of you, perhaps that is a normal, solo activity.

This is one of those dates I don't mind repeating over and over. I hope you will enjoy it too. It's meant to be filled with fun and enjoyed with the Best Friend any of us could ever ask for.

Date 21
Rockin' Karaoke

Location: A private place
Supplies: A computer, Internet.
Reading: Read chapter during your date

*A*round the time of penning this chapter, my husband and I signed up to be volunteers at the Tim Tebow Foundation's *Night to Shine*. A local church hosts this event annually, a prom for some incredibly special people. We were assigned to work the karaoke room.

Those prom kings and queens know how to sing with abandon. The most touching song to hear them sing was *This is Me* from the film, *The Greatest Showman*. You could see the lyrics speaking to their spirits and building their self-esteem.

In a prior installment, I suggested a Serenade Date. That was a bit different. A more subdued, yet no less important, love song to our Lord.

On this one, I want you to get your "rock the night away" spirit on. Full fledged, all out fun that karaoke is supposed to be. (I may or may not have belted out a country song at *Night to Shine* before our room got busy.)

You'd possibly be making a fool of yourself, except if you do this right and you're home alone, it won't matter. No one will hear you but Jesus. (Unless you live super close to your neighbors.) And He'll enjoy every minute of it, even if you are out of tune, out of sync, and can't sing a note. It doesn't matter.

I suggest for this you choose a fun, kicky, upbeat number. But also one that has a spiritual theme or song to our Lord. (Unlike my country song at *Night to Shine*.)

I will include a short list of suggestions. Like the Serenade Date, see if you can find the lyrics online (either on YouTube or on a lyric website, so you can officially sing along.)

So many ministries and music groups these days upload lyric videos. It should be easy to find a song you like. (What I wouldn't have given, to have had access to that when I was a kid! Not only to choose my favorite song, on demand, but know all the words.)

So get ready to sing for Jesus. Dance around if you want to. This isn't the ballad version of this date.

You certainly don't have to confine yourself to my list here, but I'm giving some suggestions to get you started. You don't have to find YouTube videos without the artist singing like we usually do in karaoke. Feel free to sing along with them if you'd prefer.

Suggested karaoke songs:

Get Back Up — Toby Mac
I Just Need You — Toby Mac
The Great Adventure — Steven Curtis Chapman
Priceless — For King & Country
You Found Me — Switchfoot
God's Not Dead — Newsboys
You Say — Lauren Daigle
Light of the World — Lauren Daigle
Here Again — Elevation Worship
Mended — Matthew West
Strong Enough — Matthew West
All of Creation — MercyMe
The Secret Place — Phil Wickham
Surrounded (Fight My Battles) — Upper Room
Who I'm Meant to Be — Anthem Lights
King of my Heart — Steffany Gretzinger
Only Jesus — Casting Crowns
Jesus You're Beautiful — Jason Upton
Overcomer — Mandisa

Feel free to choose your favorite, fast songs to sing to our Savior. And enjoy it! Laugh, dance around, be free to praise.

Sing more than one song. Make a night of it. Enjoy every moment of showering love and affection on Jesus.

Date 22
Out of the Mouths of Babes

Location: TBD

Supplies: TBD

Reading: Read chapter before your date

The *Dates With God* experience is meant to be shared, taught to others, passed along. This includes the younger generations.

Do you have children you'd like to introduce the idea of going on dates with God to? If not, how about a niece or a nephew or the child of a close friend?

If you have more than one kid, consider taking one out at a time so you can really focus and pour into that one child.

It's never too early to start teaching children good spiritual habits. There's no reason dates with our Lord should be reserved for adults only.

Like Proverbs 22:6 reminds us, "Start children off on the way they should go, and even when they are old they will not turn from it."

I also love the famous verse from Matthew 19:14, "Jesus said, 'Let the little children come to me, and do not hinder them, for the kingdom of heaven belongs to such as these.'"

Jesus loves children. (Haven't we sung about that for decades?) How about investing some time into the children in your life to teach them to spend time with Jesus, to prioritize Him in their life and start forming a friendship with Jesus early on?

For this date, think of the child you want to bring with you. What activities do they enjoy? Is there a way for you to take that activity and welcome Jesus into it? Can you also bring a Bible story or prayer time into the day?

I think kids love individualized attention. Having you for an outing, all to themselves, you'll have their attention. (Especially if they are a child in a family with multiple kids.) Demonstrate for them that Jesus wants alone time with them too. Pray with them. Teach them to pray. Include fun activities.

You can choose a date you've already done that you think the child would enjoy, like the painting rocks date, or come up with something brand new.

I'm not choosing specific locations for this date because you know best who that child is and what they will consider fun. But some ideas may include mini-golf, a day at the beach to build sand castles, a session at a ceramic art studio. Find ways to work Jesus into the conversation and times for prayer so it's not only about the activity. Make sure they realize you are introducing them to the idea of going on a date with Jesus. Share with them some examples from your own dating life with Jesus and why you want to share that with them.

Even give them space to pray alone, like for example, sitting by a brook, with you nearby but separately having your own prayer time. Use your prayer time to pray for them.

Communion With God Ministries recommends a book for teaching kids how to journal and write out their prayers called *Children, Can You Hear Me?* by Brad Jersak. Consider using a resource like that with them as well. The earlier they learn and understand that Jesus wants to spend time with them, the better.

If you need to spend a "date in" due to weather, consider coloring books with Jesus themes. You can do one for adults while the child does one with more kid friendly drawings.

Another fun activity with kids could be teaching them sign language for songs about Jesus, getting them to perform those with you and sing along or dance. Do the kid version of karaoke with kid friendly, Christian songs. Play a game of charades using Bible stories as phrases you have to guess.

Maybe even welcome the child to help you decide on an activity they'd enjoy doing with you and Jesus. They may have some creative ideas.

Enjoy this time, as this season in their lives is fleeting. I have no doubt Jesus is pleased with us when we take time to invest in children this way.

Date 23
Reader's Choice

Location: Your choice
Supplies: Your choice
Reading: Read whole chapter before your date

*H*as this third installment of the *Dates With God* series given you new ideas for dates with Jesus that I haven't suggested? Now is the time to go on one of those.

Even if you wrote a list when going through the first two installments, write another list now or add to the one you already started. It could be a new date from this book sparked fresh ideas for you. Choose one to go on now.

What do you need to make this date happen? Will it be inside, outside, at home, or at some destination?

In any dating relationship, we enjoy sometimes letting our dates plan the outing. This is your chance to choose.

What do you want to ask Jesus to do with you today?

Think about your interests, hobbies, and resources, and turn those into dates. You know the area where you live best. You may come up with ideas that I would never think of because I don't live where you do.

Go on your creative date. Take selfies and then, if you're willing, post about it with the #dateswithGod label on social media, like Twitter or Instagram. (If you use Twitter you can tag us at @purplepenworks so we can find your post.) You can also go to our website:

www.dateswithGod.com

Leave a comment on the page for Volume Three of this series.

Feel free to just share your experience in a comment, or give us a link to where you've either blogged about your date or posted photos. By doing so, you will encourage others who are also dating God or Jesus to have even more fun than they've had so far by following my ideas. I don't pretend to be able to come up with every idea under the sun that we could enjoy on dates with God and Jesus. So I want to welcome you into this process.

So, that's it. Easy enough, right? Write that list and take a date from your list of ideas. In the future, revisit that list and try them all at least once. Repeat your favorites.

And share with us how it goes!

Date 24
Scrapbooking Your Dates

Location: A place at home with a large table or desk

Supplies: A journal, your camera, computer, pictures from your dates, a scrapbook and supplies, or an online scrapbooking program

Reading: Read whole chapter before your date

We are getting close to the end of this third volume. I hope this will be an ongoing practice. I believe we should be dating God and Jesus for the rest of our lives.

If you went through Volume One and Volume Two, you already have some sort of scrapbook to commemorate your dates.

Before you get to the final date, where you will

do a relationship check-in with God, I'd like you to use this date as a "look back" on all the dates you've been on in Volume Three. I've encouraged you along the way to take pictures. Pictures of things He's shown you, pictures of His beautiful artistry, selfies of you on dates. And in the case of this volume, which had less nature dates, I encouraged you to take photos of other things to commemorate your time, like your special ring or piece of jewelry or your feet. (Come on, now. I shared my photo. The beach version of foot washing, anyway.)

Gather all of these pictures. Now it's time to add them to whatever scrapbook you started before. This date may take a few days or a week or so because it is a project.

As a reminder, just in case you didn't start that scrapbook yet, there are various approaches to this date you can take. You can choose to scrapbook your dates in a real live scrapbook with stickers and decorations. You can use a journaling photo album. You can start a blog about your dates, complete with photos. Or you can put together an online scrapbook. Either way, this is meant to be a faith-building exercise.

This project will continue to chronicle all the time you've spent with God since this journey began. Once you choose your method for scrapbooking, label your photos with what Date number they were from out of this book, if you haven't already.

Remember to look up words in your journal that you sensed Jesus speaking to you on each date. Pick out a special quote or piece of wisdom you feel He showed you on each date that goes with the pictures.

By now, you have probably had 23 new experiences with Jesus that you haven't had before (Hopefully to add to the other 50). Save them and capture those memories.

Like any dating relationship, looking back on where we've been and the good times we've had is a fun activity. Especially if you have built good memories together. This date helps you do this visually. The next date will get into having some concentrated chat time with Jesus to check in on your relationship.

Meanwhile, as you work through this project, I hope you enjoy your trip down memory lane.

Date 25
Relationship Check-In

Location: A quiet place
Supplies: A journal
Reading: Read chapter during your date

Congrats on making it this far, all the way to Date 25 of Volume Three. If you also went through Volumes One and Two, that's 75 dates now! Wow.

For this date, choose any location, perhaps even your favorite location from Dates 1-24 of this volume. It's time to do one of those "relationship check-ins."

I hope you've grown even more from the time you finished Volume One and Two.

I suggest you begin this date by reading your journal entries for your first date for all three volumes. It never hurts to ask that question again: "Where are we in this relationship?"

For this particular installment, I suggested you start with a love letter to Jesus about your dreams for the next round of dates with Him.

I can promise you that if you've been participating actively in these dates, your relationship is stronger than it was 24 dates ago.

Or 49 dates ago or 74 dates ago.

You've probably grown, gotten to know more about Jesus, His wonderful attributes, His personality, and His love for you. My hope is your love for Him is exponentially greater. But it always helps to stop, check-in, and take inventory.

Remember that Jesus loves you. He's already accepted you. There's nothing to be nervous about. He is more than happy to come to the table to chat with you about your relationship. I'm sure by now your love for Him has grown stronger as well.

As you settle into your comfortable place, open your Dates With God journal.

- Do you feel closer to Jesus than you did before you went on your first date of Volume 1?
- Do you feel even closer than when you started Volume 2? Are you continuing to

progress?

- In what ways do you feel like you know Jesus better?
- What was your favorite date of the 24 in this volume? Are there any you would like to repeat?
- What was your least favorite and why? Is it worth doing over?
- Is it easier to chat with Jesus and hear His voice, the more time you spend with Him?
- In what ways did Jesus show up on dates for you during this time that you hadn't experienced before?
- What are your future goals regarding your relationship with Jesus?
- Make a plan: How would you like your dating relationship with Jesus to continue?

Next, ask Jesus a few questions and jot down anything you feel He says to you:

- Lord, how do you feel about our relationship now versus before?
- In what ways have I grown?
- Where can I improve in my quest to know you better, Lord?
- Have I let anything come between You and

me lately?
- Is there anything I'm not asking that you'd like to share with me?

Make a plan and schedule to keep going after you close this book. Naturally, you can always reread and revisit the dates in Volume 1-3. I'd just like to encourage you to make this an ongoing thing for you.

The goal of this book series is to help you establish a continuous relationship. I don't want you to finish this book (or any other volume) and stop dating God. If anything, I want this experience to have ignited a passion in you for Jesus. It's like a good meal. One you have one, you want another one once you're hungry again. And I sure hope these dates have kicked into high gear a healthy hunger for Jesus.

Hopefully, this check-in results in that mutual decision to keep dating, like Volumes 1 and 2 clearly did.

This part is *your* decision. Will you continue to invest in your love relationship? Will you continue to play your part in how much it grows?

As a reminder: Your heart is safe with Jesus. You are accepted, and you are loved and wanted.

You are not abandoned by Him. This is the safest dating relationship you can ever be in. He is your Savior and Friend.

Jesus is inviting you into a deeper love relationship with Him. Accept the hand of the Lover of your soul.

About the Author

Cheryl McKay has been professionally writing since 1997. Tommy Nelson served as her first publisher, teaming her with Frank Peretti on the *Wild and Wacky, Totally True Bible Stories* series. Cheryl wrote the screenplay adaptation of *The Ultimate Gift*, the feature film starring Academy Award Nominees James Garner and Abigail Breslin. It's based on Jim Stovall's best-selling novel. The film was released by Fox in theaters in Spring 2007 and has won such awards as the Crystal Heart Award, the Crystal Dove, one of the Top Ten Family Movies at MovieGuide Awards, and a CAMIE Award. She also wrote the DVD for *Gigi: God's Little Princess*, another book adaptation based on the book by Sheila Walsh, and episodes of *Superbook*. She wrote a half-hour drama for teenagers about high school violence, called *Taylor's Wall*, produced in Los Angeles by Family Theater Productions. After winning a fellowship, she was commissioned to write a feature script, *Greetings*

from the Flipside, for Art Within, which Rene Gutteridge and McKay released as a novel through B&H Publishing in October 2013. Her screenplay, *Never the Bride,* was adapted into a novel by Gutteridge and was released by Waterbrook Press in June 2009. The film version is in development. As one passionate for those who are losing hope in their wait to find love, she released the nonfiction version, *Finally the Bride: Finding Hope While Waiting.* She also penned her autobiography, *Finally Fearless: Journey from Panic to Peace.* She wrote the screen story for *The Ultimate Life*, the sequel to *The Ultimate Gift.* McKay also co-wrote the films *Extraordinary* and *Indivisible,* both faith-based features. Find her on Facebook, Twitter, Pinterest, or at her websites:

www.purplepenworks.com
www.finallyone.com
www.dateswithGod.com

*D*ear Readers:

Thank you for spending this time with me and more importantly with the God who loves you so much. I hope you will continue to go on many dates with God.

If this book has been helpful to you, please recommend it to your friends and family. Would you mind leaving a review online where you purchased this book to share your thoughts with others?

Also, please visit our website and share your date experiences. (**www.dateswithGod.com**)

I wish you many blessings in your quest to know your loving Heavenly Father deeper and wider and more intimately.

Blessings,

Cheryl McKay

Dates With God Series:

Volume One: *Adventures in Faith*
Volume Two: *Courting Spiritual Intimacy*
Volume Three: *Falling in Love with Jesus*

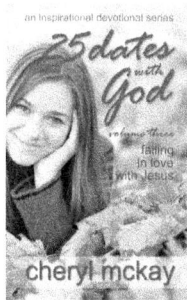

Finally
the
Bride

Finding Hope While Waiting

Cheryl McKay

Finally
Fearless

Journey from Panic to Peace

How Overcoming
Anxiety Helped Me
Find True Love

cheryl mckay

Other Books by McKay

www.ingramcontent.com/pod-product-compliance
Lightning Source LLC
Chambersburg PA
CBHW072014040426
42447CB00009B/1628